Bliss

Fraser Grace

T0347500

methuen | drama

LONDON • NEW YORK • OXFORD • NEW DELHI • SYDNEY

METHUEN DRAMA
Bloomsbury Publishing Plc
50 Bedford Square, London, WC1B 3DP, UK
1385 Broadway, New York, NY 10018, USA
29 Earlsfort Terrace, Dublin 2, Ireland

BLOOMSBURY, METHUEN DRAMA and the Methuen Drama logo are
trademarks of Bloomsbury Publishing Plc

First published in Great Britain 2021

This edition published 2022

A catalogue record for this book is available from the British Library.

A catalog record for this book is available from the Library of Congress.

ISBN: PB: 978-1-3503-4623-9
ePDF: 978-1-3503-4624-6
ePub: 978-1-3503-4625-3

Series: Modern Plays

Typeset by Mark Heslington Ltd, Scarborough, North Yorkshire

To find out more about our authors and books visit
www.bloomsbury.com and sign up for our newsletters.

Menagerie Theatre Company in association with Neil McPherson for the Finborough Theatre presents

The world premiere

Bliss

by Fraser Grace

First performance at the Finborough Theatre: Tuesday, 17 May 2022.

BLISS

by Fraser Grace

Cast in order of appearance

Nikita Firsov	**Jesse Rutherford**
Lyuba	**Bess Roche**
Tramp	**Jeremy Killick**
Zhenya	**Caroline Rippin**
Mikhail	**Patrick Morris**
Vlass	**Patrick Morris**
Paulina	**Caroline Rippin**
Investigator	**Jeremy Killick**

Russia, 1921, following the Civil War.

The approximate running time is two and a half hours.

There will be one interval of fifteen minutes.

Director and Designer	**Paul Bourne**
Composer and Sound Designer	**Michaela Polakova**
Lighting Designer and Production Manager	**Ash Day**
Producer	**Jessie Anand**
Assistant Stage Manager	**Beth Astins**

Jeremy Killick | Tramp and Investigator

Trained at Exeter University and Drama Studio London.

Productions with Menagerie include *Correspondence* (Pleasance Edinburgh).

Theatre includes *Bloody Mess* (Volksbühne, Berlin), *Tomorrow's Parties* (Sydney International Festival), *Out of Order* (Pompidou Centre, Paris), *Real Magic* (La Mama, New York), *Complete Works* (Barbican Centre and UCLA), all with Forced Entertainment. Other theatre includes *Copenhagen* (Duchess Theatre), *Booty Looting* (Théâtre de la Ville, Paris), *Talk to the Demon* (Koninklijk Vlaams Schouwburg, Brussels) and *Poseidon* (The Young Vic).

Films include lead roles in *Galloping Mind, Second Spring* and *Monkey Sandwich*.

Television includes *Quiz* and *The Fear Index*.

Patrick Morris | Mikhail and Vlass

Trained at Exeter University and San Francisco Mime Troupe.

Theatre includes *The Unleashing of Leopold Bloom* (formerly *bloominauschwitz*), winner of Best New Play (Brighton Fringe), *Out of Your Knowledge* (Pleasance Edinburgh), *Frobisher's Gold* (Shaw Theatre), *Hard Sell* (National and International Tour), *Medea* and *Pushing Daisies* (Foursight Theatre), *Top Secret* (New International Encounter), *Henry VI* (Public Theatre of New York), *Counting the Ways* (New York), *Springtime*, *Oscar and Bertha* and *Drowning* (Magic Theatre, San Francisco).

Patrick is Co-Artistic Director of Menagerie and has directed and developed work with Fraser Grace, Steve Waters, Naomi Wallace, Tom Stoppard, Claire MacDonald, Hisham Matar and Maria Irene Fornes among many others.

Caroline Rippin | Paulina and Zhenya

Trained at Bretton Hall.

Theatre includes *Phenomenon* (Menagerie and Cambridge Junction), *The Great Austerity Debate* (National Tour), *What Country, Friends, Is This?* (Hotbed Festival), *The Summer Before Everything* (Oxford

Playhouse), *Pictures of You* (Soho Theatre), *A Workhouse Christmas* (Jumped Up Theatre), *Let Newton Be* (Menagerie), *Four for Jericho* (Cambridge Junction), *Stand By Your Van* (Pleasance Edinburgh), *A Sudden Visitation of Calamity* (Hotbed Festival and Soho Theatre), *Frobisher's Gold* (Shaw Theatre), *Stormin' Jack Norman* (Theatre503), *Michelle and The Landlady* (National Tour for Menagerie), *Motherf**ker Island* and *In the White Highlands* (Cambridge Drama Centre), *Blagger* (Teatro Piccolo), *Peer Gynt* (Wakefield Opera House) and *White Nights* (The Spot).

Direction includes *Fallible* (Menagerie and Cambridge Junction), *Doghead Boy and Sharkmouth Go To Ikea*, *Blacklight* and *Oran's Message* (Menagerie) and *Return Of The Vanishing Peasant* (Mercury Theatre, Colchester).

Bess Roche | Lyuba

Trained at The Royal Central School of Speech and Drama.

Theatre includes *Love, No Country* (Menagerie and Cambridge Junction), *Legless* (Southwark Playhouse and Theatre503), *Precieuses Ridicules* (Cockpit Theatre), and *The Bacchanals* (Etcetera Theatre and Edinburgh Festival).

Jesse Rutherford | Nikita

Trained at Rose Bruford.

Theatre includes *Bed Seven* (Seven Dials Playhouse), *Cornermen* (National Tour), *Goody* (Greenwich Theatre and Pleasance Edinburgh), *Luna Park* (Soho Theatre and Zoo, Edinburgh) and *Chicken Shop* (Park Theatre). Understudy roles include *A Number* (Bridge Theatre) and *Killer Joe* (Trafalgar Studios).

Television includes *Masters of the Air*, *Locked Up Abroad*, *EastEnders, Doctors* and *Halcyon*.

Voiceover work includes *Nail Bomber: Manhunt*.

Fraser Grace | Playwright

Fraser Grace's first play *Perpetua* was joint winner of the Verity Bargate Award, and his best-known work, *Breakfast with Mugabe*, was premiered by the Royal Shakespeare Company in the Swan Theatre, Stratford–Upon-Avon, where it won the John Whiting Award for Best New Play and a Silver Sony Award when broadcast on BBC Radio 3 and the World Service – all directed by Antony Sher. *Breakfast with Mugabe* has since been revived in the UK and in the USA, where it was again shortlisted Off-Broadway for The Broadway Alliance Award for Best Play. His other plays include *Always Orange* (The Other Place, Stratford-Upon-Avon), *Kalashnikov: In the Woods by the Lake* (National Tour), *Tongues* (Menagerie National Tour), *King David Man of Blood* (Mercury Theatre, Colchester), *The Lifesavers*, nominated for TMA award for Best New Play (Mercury Theatre, Colchester, and Theatre503), *Frobisher's Gold* with Janet Suzman (Shaw Theatre), *Who Killed Mr Drum* (Riverside Studios), *Gifts of War* (Menagerie at Theatre503), and *Perpetua*, joint winner of the Verity Bargate Award (Soho Theatre and Birmingham Rep).

Paul Bourne | Director and Designer

Paul Bourne is Artistic Director of Menagerie in Cambridge and Co-Artistic Director of Divadlo 6–16 (Prague). Direction and Designing includes *Frobisher's Gold* (Shaw Theatre), *Stand By Your Van* (Pleasance Edinburgh), *Egusi Soup* (Soho Theatre, Birmingham Rep and Nottingham Playhouse), *Out of Your Knowledge* (National Tour), *Swimming* (Pleasance Edinburgh), *In The White Highlands* (Soho Theatre), *Hard Sell* (Theatre503 and Jatka 78, Prague), *Animal Farm* (Voronezh Theatre, Russia) and *Correspondence* (Jatka 78, Prague).

Ash Day | Lighting Designer

Trained at Liverpool Institute for Performing Arts.

Ash started his career working as a session bass player, touring with theatre shows including *Rent* (National Tour 2001) and *Fame* (National Tour 2003), before working behind the scenes as a lighting technician and designer. He has toured around the world with several music, dance and theatre productions, at venues as varied as the Royal Albert Hall, The Kremlin in Moscow, Glastonbury, and Red Rocks Amphitheatre in Colorado.

He was lighting designer for artists including Joan Armatrading, Albert Hammond, Paul Potts, Wild Women Blues, Tango Pasion, and Rasta Thomas' *Bad Boys of Dance: Rock the Ballet*.

He now works mainly in Cambridge as a technician, set builder, sound designer, lighting designer and production manager for various theatre companies, including the Cambridge Junction, New International Encounter and Menagerie Theatre Company.

Michaela Polakova | Composer

Michaela Polakova is a Czech-born composer, singer, songwriter and pianist based in Essex.

Trained at Prague Conservatoire, University of East London and King's College London.

Theatre Composition includes *The Night Before the Funeral* (?vanda Theatre, Prague).

Theatre as a performer includes *Excalibur* (Ta Fantastika, Prague).

Short Film Composition includes *Lurker*.

Michaela has released several albums with Sony Music BMG. In 2016 she released the critically acclaimed album *Ellis Island* through Warner Music, recorded with singer and friend Natalie Kocab, featuring Nick McCabe (The Verve) on guitar and Fernando Saunders (Lou Reed) on bass.

Production Acknowledgements

Initial Casting Consultancy	**Liv Barr**
PR	**Mobius**
Graphic Design	**Geoff Shirley**

 menagerie

Since 2000, Menagerie has been nurturing, developing and producing new writing for the stage. From our base at Cambridge Junction we have worked with hundreds of playwrights to put their work in front of audiences. Always open to new forms, ideas and challenges, we produce plays which explore the diverse ways in which the human spirit survives and thrives.

We tour regionally, nationally and internationally: to venues in Cambridge, London, Edinburgh and Dublin, but also further afield in Germany, Turkey, Russia, Serbia, the USA and India. We produce work by writers including Steve Waters, Fraser Grace, Naomi Wallace, Craig Baxter, Janice Okoh and Jane Upton. We work with leading academics as part of our Ideas Stage, collaborating with institutions such as the University of Cambridge, University College London and Queen Mary University. We also run innovative community projects in and around Cambridge. At the heart of our mission is a passion for new writing and a commitment to the writers that create it.

You can find out more about us on www.menagerietheatre.co.uk.

FINBOROUGH THEATRE

"Probably the most influential fringe theatre in the world." *Time Out*

"Not just a theatre, but a miracle." *Metro*

"The mighty little Finborough which, under Neil McPherson, continues to offer a mixture of neglected classics and new writing in a cannily curated mix." Lyn Gardner, *The Stage*

"The tiny but mighty Finborough"
Ben Brantley, *The New York Times*

Founded in 1980, the multi-award-winning Finborough Theatre presents plays and music theatre, concentrated exclusively on vibrant new writing and unique rediscoveries from the 19th and 20th centuries, both in our 154 year old home and online through our #FinboroughFrontier digital initiative.

Our programme is unique – we never present work that has been seen anywhere in London during the last 25 years. Behind the scenes, we continue to discover and develop a new generation of theatre makers.

Despite remaining completely unsubsidised, the Finborough Theatre has an unparalleled track record for attracting the finest talent who go on to become leading voices in British theatre. Under Artistic Director Neil McPherson, it has discovered some of the UK's most exciting new playwrights including Laura Wade, James Graham, Mike Bartlett, Jack Thorne, Nicholas de Jongh and Anders Lustgarten, and directors including Tamara Harvey, Robert Hastie, Blanche McIntyre, Kate Wasserberg and Sam Yates.

Artists working at the theatre in the 1980s included Clive Barker, Rory Bremner, Nica Burns, Kathy Burke, Ken Campbell, Jane Horrocks and Claire Dowie. In the 1990s, the Finborough Theatre first became known for new writing including Naomi Wallace's first play *The War Boys*, Rachel Weisz in David Farr's *Neville Southall's Washbag*, four plays by Anthony Neilson including *Penetrator* and *The Censor*, both of which transferred to the Royal Court Theatre, and new plays by Richard Bean, Lucinda Coxon, David Eldridge and Tony Marchant. New writing development included the premieres of modern classics such as Mark Ravenhill's

*Shopping and F***king*, Conor McPherson's *This Lime Tree Bower*, Naomi Wallace's *Slaughter City* and Martin McDonagh's *The Pillowman*.

Since 2000, new British plays have included Laura Wade's London debut *Young Emma*, commissioned for the Finborough Theatre, James Graham's *Albert's Boy* with Victor Spinetti, Sarah Grochala's *S27*, Athena Stevens' *Schism* which was nominated for an Olivier Award, and West End transfers for Joy Wilkinson's *Fair*, Nicholas de Jongh's *Plague Over England*, Jack Thorne's *Fanny and Faggot*, Neil McPherson's Olivier Award nominated *It Is Easy To Be Dead*, and Dawn King's *Foxfinder*.

UK premieres of foreign plays have included plays by Brad Fraser, Lanford Wilson, Larry Kramer, Tennessee Williams, Suzan-Lori Parks, Jordan Tannahill, the English premieres of two Scots language classics by Robert McLellan, and West End transfers for Frank McGuinness' *Gates of Gold* with William Gaunt and John Bennett, and Craig Higginson's *Dream of the Dog* with Dame Janet Suzman.

Rediscoveries of neglected work – most commissioned by the Finborough Theatre – have included the first London revivals of Rolf Hochhuth's *Soldiers* and *The Representative*, both parts of Keith Dewhurst's *Lark Rise to Candleford*, *Etta Jenks* with Clarke Peters and Daniela Nardini, Noël Coward's first play *The Rat Trap*, Lennox Robinson's *Drama at Inish* with Celia Imrie and Paul O'Grady, and Emlyn Williams' *Accolade*, and John Van Druten's *London Wall* (both of which transferred to St James' Theatre), and J. B. Priestley's *Cornelius* which transferred to a sell-out Off Broadway run in New York City.

Music Theatre has included the new (premieres from Craig Adams, Grant Olding, Charles Miller, Michael John LaChiusa, Adam Guettel, Andrew Lippa, Paul Scott Goodman, and Adam Gwon's *Ordinary Days* which transferred to the West End) and the old (the UK premiere of Rodgers and Hammerstein's *State Fair* which also transferred to the West End), and the acclaimed 'Celebrating British Music Theatre' series.

The Finborough Theatre won the 2020 London Pub Theatres Pub Theatre of the Year Award, *The Stage* Fringe Theatre of the Year Award in 2011, *London Theatre Reviews'* Empty Space Peter Brook Award in 2010 and 2012, swept the board with eight awards at the 2012 OffWestEnd Awards, and was nominated for an Olivier Award in 2017 and 2019. Artistic Director Neil McPherson was awarded the Critics' Circle Special Award for Services to Theatre in 2019. It is the only unsubsidised theatre ever to be awarded the Channel 4 Playwrights Scheme bursary eleven times.

www.finboroughtheatre.co.uk

FINBOROUGH THEATRE

118 Finborough Road, London SW10 9ED
admin@finboroughtheatre.co.uk
www.finboroughtheatre.co.uk

Artistic Director | **Neil McPherson**
Founding Director | **Phil Willmott**
Resident Designer | **Alex Marker**
General Manager | **Matilda Russell**
Playwrights in Residence | **James Graham, Dawn King, Anders Lustgarten, Hannah Morley, Carmen Nasr, Shamser Sinha, Athena Stevens** and **Chris Thompson**
Playwright on Attachment | **Abigail Andjel**
Technical Manager | **Angus Chisholm**
Literary Manager | **Sue Healy**
Deputy Literary Manager | **Rhys Hayes**
Literary Assistants | **Sibylla Kalid, Alice Chambers, Ella Fidler** and **Ella Gold**
Literary Assistants (International) | **Serena Haywood** and **Sian Rowland**
Associate Producer | **Arsalan Sattari**
Associate Sound Designer | **Julian Starr**
Book Keeper | **Patti Williams**
Board of Trustees | **Felix Cassel, Gordon Hopkinson, Russell Levinson, Rebecca Maltby, Alice Pakenham, Antonella Petrancosta** and **Paul Webster**
And our volunteers.

The Finborough Theatre is a member of the Independent Theatre Council, the Society of Independent Theatres, Musical Theatre Network, The Friends of Brompton Cemetery and The Earl's Court Society, and supports #time4change's Mental Health Charter.

Supported by

The Theatres Trust Theatres Protection Fund Small Grants Programme, supported by The Linbury Trust

The Finborough Theatre receives no regular funding from the Royal Borough of Kensington and Chelsea.

Mailing
Email admin@finboroughtheatre.co.uk or give your details to our Box Office staff to join our free email list.

Playscripts
Many of the Finborough Theatre's plays have been published and are on sale from our website.

Local History
The Finborough Theatre's local history website is online at **www.earlscourtlocalhistory.co.uk**

On Social Media
www.facebook.com/FinboroughTheatre

www.twitter.com/finborough

www.instagram.com/finboroughtheatre

www.youtube.com/user/finboroughtheatre

Friends
The Finborough Theatre is a registered charity. We receive no public funding, and rely solely on the support of our audiences. Please do consider supporting us by becoming a member of our Friends of the Finborough Theatre scheme. There are four categories of Friends, each offering a wide range of benefits.

Smoking is not permitted in the auditorium.
The videotaping or making of electronic or other audio and/or visual recordings or streams of this production is strictly prohibited.
PLEASE BE CONSIDERATE OF OTHERS, AND WEAR A FACE COVERING FULLY COVERING YOUR MOUTH AND NOSE FOR THE DURATION OF THE PERFORMANCE.

In accordance with the requirements of the Royal Borough of Kensington and Chelsea:
1. The public may leave at the end of the performance by all doors and such doors must at that time be kept open.
2. All gangways, corridors, staircases and external passageways intended for exit shall be left entirely free from obstruction whether permanent or temporary.
3. Persons shall not be permitted to stand or sit in any of the gangways intercepting the seating or to sit in any of the other gangways.
The Finborough Theatre is a registered charity and a company limited by guarantee. Registered in England and Wales no. 3448268. Registered Charity no. 1071304. Registered Office: 118 Finborough Road, London SW10 9ED.

Bliss

Characters

Nikita Firsov, *a returning soldier*
Lyuba, *a student of medicine*
Zhenya, *her fellow student, vivacious friend and food supply*
Dad, *Nikita's father, a joiner*
Vlass, *the watchman-supervisor*
Paulina, *the watchman's wife*
Investigator, *a member of the militia*

Other parts

Schoolteacher, **Tramp**, **Market Trader** *played by members of the cast*

Place

Part One – 'an obscure provincial town' on the River Potudan.

Part Two – the same, and in Kantemirovka, a market town some distance away.

Time

The action begins in 1921, a time of famine after the Russian Civil War.

Note on text

The play is based on 'The River Potudan', a short story by Andrey Platonov, read in a translation by Robert and Elizabeth Chandler and Angela Livingstone.

Note on performance

The play may be performed by five actors, with the following doubling:

Nikita Firsov
Lyuba
Zhenya / Paulina
Dad / Vlass
Investigator / Tramp
All other characters played by the cast

Prologue

Weak sunshine.

Stage is preset with a small card table. The **Schoolteacher** *sits, back to audience, or half-on, playing patience.*

Offstage, someone is practising a piano piece – not a very good player. Occasionally the **Schoolteacher** *calls out to her pupil, 'Again . . .!' or 'Not so fast, Lyuba, adante'.*

Eventually, the **Schoolteacher** *sighs and scrapes up the cards.*

Schoolteacher   Enough, Lyuba. No more.

Off, piano lid is slammed shut. The **Schoolteacher** *folds away the table and exits. Lights change.*

Part One

One

Nikita *is waiting in the street, late afternoon. He wears a greatcoat, but looks gaunt, his hair long and lank. A young woman approaches – **Lyuba** – poorly dressed, and even more gaunt than **Nikita**. Her shoes are tied up with string, and she carries a pile of books.*

*When **Lyuba** sees **Nikita**, she stops short.*

Lyuba   You.

Pause.

Nikita (*prompting*)   Nikita.

Lyuba   Nikita, of course.

Nikita   You are Lyuba.

Lyuba   I know.

Pause.

Lyuba   How long have you been . . . (waiting)?

When did you get back, Nikita?

Nikita   Yesterday. Today.

Lyuba   Today. Now you're here, in our street.

Nikita   I had to register with the Commissariat, for the reserve. I kept walking.

He looks up at the house.

I came to this house before.

Courting the schoolteacher.

Lyuba   ?

Nikita   There was furniture. A wardrobe, a clock, cups, a piano . . .

Lyuba   You courted my mother?

Beat.

Nikita   Dad courted her. I was fourteen.

Lyuba   Of course. Old Mikhail with his oiled hair.

And the young one, Nikita Firsov.

Nikita   No point coming back after that. 'They have nice things – what would we talk about?'

That was . . . (a long time ago).

Good day, comrade.

He makes to exit.

Lyuba   Mother passed two winters ago. I tried to keep the piano, but I had to feed the stove.

Nikita   I'm sorry for your trouble, Lyuba.

She nods acknowledgement.

Nikita   I don't miss the piano.

Smiles. Pause.

Lyuba   Your father, is he . . .? Are you . . .

Nikita   Both of us. Alive.

Lyuba   Good. You came home to someone.

Beat.

Nikita   We didn't even know it was over. 'Go back to whatever godforsaken places you come from.' We had a smoke, said goodbyes. I started walking.

Now I am here, speaking to you.

Lyuba   You walked all the way?

How did you know where to go?

Nikita   I followed the river.

Lyuba   It's miles!

Nikita   I kept to the river.

Lyuba   You must have walked for weeks!

Beat.

You smell very badly, Nikita.

Pause.

Nikita   What sort of life do you have, Lyuba? Have you a place, in the new world? A job . . .?

Lyuba   I'm a student. (*The books.*) Medicine.

Nikita   Ah. Pity.

Lyuba   ?

Nikita   No doctors needed now. Too late for the dead, the living are healed.

Beat.

Lyuba   Are you?

Nikita *puts on his cap.*

Nikita   It's good to see you're alive, Lyuba. Good to know not all the ghosts in the street are enemies.

Again, he makes to exit. She makes a decision.

Lyuba   Come in, Nikita. Now you're here.

See the house again.

Beat. She exits. He waits, takes his hat off again, sniffs himself, follows, the action continues as smoothly as possible, into . . .

Two

Lights up on **Lyuba**'*s house.*

A bed, a very tatty piano stool and downstage – a wood-burning stove. Somewhere a clock. **Lyuba** *puts her books down on the bed, takes pins from her hair.*

Lyuba   How are you at lighting stoves? I use the small one now; that burns with a few sticks.

He sets about it. She feels the cold, and watches him.

Lyuba   The cold's like some guest you can't get rid of.

The furniture came in useful that way. So much has gone!

There's still the clock; that doesn't work.

You need a knack with a stove like that.

Nikita   We fixed a lot of things in the war. Roofs, fences –

The unit I was with, we built a whole bridge for a village in the Altai region.

The Whites fought for the old things. We knew it's the future that counts.

(*The stove.*) You're right, it's tricky.

Lyuba   Do you have food in your pockets, Nikita?

Nikita *hasn't any food.*

Lyuba   My friend Zhenya comes round in the evenings. She brings food from home, so I can think. Her father commands the division.

It's nice to be talked to, to study.

I suppose she's not coming.

Her eyes fall again on his pockets.

Lyuba   No use thinking of food. I have to lie down. When I sleep for a while the pains pass over. That's usually how I manage.

Will you stay, for a while, while I sleep?

You can keep the place warm, keep the stove lit, I can rest.

Would you do that for me, Nikita?

Beat.

Nikita   Yes.

I'll sit here, in the chair. Guard duty.

Lyuba   Mikhail won't miss you, will he, your father?

Nikita   Dad? No. He survived a long while on his own.

Some people get used to it.

I don't think anyone can do anything good on their own.

That's why we need comrades.

She smiles, turns back the bed, then gets into the bed fully dressed, all the time talking, rubbing her feet.

Lyuba   My toes have been talking to my stomach. They don't tell you about that in medical books. There must be a theory – how one part of the body sets off aches in another.

I should propose a theory myself, be my own proof.

I'm fine once the pain's gone off, I can concentrate.

Perhaps you'd talk for me, comrade, so I can sleep.

Nikita   ?

Lyuba   I like to hear people.

Sometimes I bang pots together in the kitchen, just for the noise. It must sound strange, I suppose.

Nikita   Enough to drive the neighbours out.

What subject should I address?

Lyuba   Tell me what you've seen, what you've noticed in the world.

I'll know what to expect, when I qualify.

(*Without irony.*) You mustn't be ashamed, comrade, of the work you've done in the war.

If there was no victory, we'd have no kind of life. Not even this.

He nods his thanks. Clears his throat.

Nikita   What I've seen.

Pause.

There's not so many people now.

A lot of houses are empty, not much traffic in the lanes . . .

Burials: there'll be a lot of those in the spring.

Some people died in the fighting, but the ground was too hard: the earth refused to welcome the dead.

It'll thaw soon, a spade will do it.

Some of the old people . . . shock kept them going. Now it's over, they let go, surrender their grip.

I wouldn't want to live in a city now. There are bagmen on the trains, they come out to the country with their heirlooms and wedding rings, begging for loaves or a scrap of meat.

There's no harvest in the fields. The seed was requisitioned.

Nothing to plant next year, nothing to eat now . . .

Sorry. I shouldn't talk about food.

I don't eat much. Don't sleep. I march. A model soldier.

There was one time I slept, walking home.

I dreamed there was a creature, a furry little thing – some mouse or dormouse, it climbed into me, lay down in my mouth. Grown fat from chewing nothing but wheat. Settled down inside me for a good old snooze.

It was so furry and warm it made me choke, the more I choked the more it burrowed down, got into my lungs, in my heart.

In the end it got out by itself. Ran away terrified, poor thing. I woke up, hot with fever, and this tramp stepped right over me. He didn't stop, or speak – just stepped over me – as if I was a branch, or a puddle. The kind of puddle you wash your face in, then wait for it to settle. See yourself.

I followed after him, after that, the tramp, all the way to the edge of town. He was coming my way, lucky for me. Coming to the old place, to Dad's house. To you, Lyuba.

Pause. **Lyuba** *is asleep.*

Nikita   I don't know what kind of life is possible now, what place there'll be for me. Who knows what's coming next?

That's why the new world has to begin; to fix us down, all those who survived, fix us in place.

Sleep. You've mastered a lost craft there. A lost craft, bobbing off, down river.

Pause.

He gets up and crosses to the bed. **Nikita** *stands gazing at the sleeping* **Lyuba**.

He bends towards her – and pulls the blanket up around her shoulders.

The stumbling piano music returns. He returns to the chair. Offstage, dogs bark.

Nikita   I'll stay here.

He gazes into the fire. Lights.

Three

The same. The bed is empty. A light shines off, upstage right – perhaps over a door – suggesting this is where **Lyuba** *might be, in the washroom.*

Having discarded his coat and rolled up his sleeves, **Nikita** *is banking up the stove with a bucket full of wood shavings and twigs.*

Zhenya (*off, calling*)   Looby? . . . Hello?

Zhenya *enters* **Nikita** *twists to see her, and stands almost to attention.*

Nikita   You. You must be . . . (*He dredges up the name.*) Zhenya.

Zhenya   Must I?

Nikita   Lyuba said you came.

Zhenya   And you are . . .?

Nikita*'s confidence could easily crumble.*

Nikita   Firsov. Nikita. A friend to Lyuba, from before.

She proffers her hand, and shakes his.

Zhenya   Pleased to meet you, Nikita Firsov.

She puts down her bag, pulls off her gloves.

Zhenya   Show me your hands again, will you? Don't worry, I won't steal them.

He obeys, apologetically.

Nikita   There's a lot of dirt, from the stove . . . and also . . .

She coughs.

Zhenya   Sorry.

Recovering, she takes his hands in hers, turns them over, examines them and smiles to herself, satisfied. She releases them and refers to the stove.

Zhenya   You should light the big stove. If Lyuba doesn't stay warm, she'll get ill. We should find her more clothes too; that dress she's been wearing is so thin it looks like a shroud, don't you think?

Nikita   I . . . don't know what to say.

Zhenya   How long have you been here Nikita Firsov?

Nikita   I sat in the chair, while Lyuba rested.

Zhenya   You're staying for good, are you? In the town?

Enter **Lyuba** *from the washroom.*

Lyuba   Zhenya – I thought it must be you!

Zhenya   Lyushka!

They embrace and kiss with girlish excitement.

Lyuba   It's good to see you. Did you bring the books?
The histology?

Zhenya   The library was closed by the time I got out . . .
Papa wanted his dinner, screaming for it, I couldn't get away.

Sorry.

Lyuba   It doesn't matter. I memorised the first chapter at
the academy. I'll recite it if you like, you can write it down for
both of us. Will that work, do you think?

Zhenya   It's worked before, we could try.

Beat.

Lyuba   Did you bring food, Zhenya? If you haven't it
doesn't matter, only . . .

Zhenya   There's some. It's just a few leftovers. Everyone
wants to clear their plate these days.

She glances anxiously toward **Nikita** *– if he stays there'll be less food
to go round.*

Lyuba   This is Nikita Firsov.

Zhenya   Yes, we've met.

Lyuba   He's back from the front. Nikita walked the whole
way, from the fighting.

Nikita   The fighting was over.

Zhenya   A soldier. Of course. I should have seen that.

Nikita   I'm a joiner. Then I joined the army.

Zhenya   Congratulations, comrade. You and your fellows made the world a more spacious place, with all the killing.

Beat.

Lyuba   Zhenya's brothers . . . One of them died – one is still missing.

Nikita   But her father's a soldier. The commander.

Zhenya   Some people survive, that's all.

Beat.

Nikita   My own brothers fell in the last war, the Patriotic War. This was the last war ever, they say.

Zhenya   We have to study – then we can be useful to the ones who are left. That's the purpose of women, did you know? To fill the spaces made by men.

Father says no one has a use for soldiers now – there'll have to be another war, to clear up the streets.

Beat.

Nikita   I'll get off, then.

He takes his coat and makes to leave. Without receiving a response from **Zhenya**.

Nikita   It was a pleasure to meet you, comrades.

It was a pleasure to meet you, Zhenya.

Lyuba.

Still no response from **Zhenya**. *He again makes to exit, only to be stopped by* **Lyuba**.

Lyuba   Nikita – you won't forget me will you? Now you know where I am.

Nikita   I won't. I've no one else to remember.

He exits.

Zhenya   Eat first, then study. I've only got potatoes. Want them?

Lyuba   Yes. Please.

Zhenya   Still warm, a little.

Lyuba   Thank you, Zhenya.

They sit close to the stove, unwrap the potatoes from a cloth, and **Lyuba** *begins to eat.* **Zhenya** *signals that she needs no food, then coughs heavily.* **Lyuba** *waits.*

Lyuba   Alright?

Zhenya   Fine. He's a gloomy one, your soldier. Handsome though, if he was cleaned up.

Lyuba   He's not a soldier really.

He's not *my* soldier, anyway.

Zhenya *coughs again.*

Lyuba   Have a drink, Zhenya. You'll choke.

Zhenya   He's been at war, what's that if not a soldier?

Lyuba   Just a man in uniform, you know that. He's a carpenter.

Zhenya   He can't be a proper soldier, it's true. He has a long life ahead of him.

Lyuba   ?

Zhenya   I read his palm.

Lyuba   Zhenya, you're supposed to be a scientist!

Zhenya   Embrace the new, keep the best of the old. His other hand is scarred – you've no idea what's going on there. It's the first palm that counts, anyway.

You're lucky, Lyushka. To find a man that will live a long life, that's every woman's dream.

Lyuba   Most women say the opposite. All the women I know can't say a good word about their husbands.

Zhenya   Ha – You're in love already!

Lyuba   What?

Zhenya   You said 'husband'.

Lyuba   I did. He's only been here a few hours.

Zhenya   A few hours in your bed.

Lyuba   I was sleeping. Nikita watched for me.

Zhenya   A man only needs five minutes to drum up a passion. Only makes it last two, usually.

Lyuba   Zhenya, please!

Zhenya   You should hear what they say in the army; a woman's sex is a glass of water for a thirsty comrade.

Lyuba   Why do you repeat these things? Come on, we have to start work.

Zhenya   Oh, let's talk for a while first, seems like days since we had a good gossip.

She loosens her clothing, feeling the fever.

Lyuba   Zhenya, are you unwell?

Zhenya   I'm fine.

I give in. You said it yourself, while there's light, we work.

Otherwise food, lamp oil, it's a waste. Do you have a pencil, Looby?

Lyuba   Somewhere . . . It's not new . . .

She finds it.

If you're sure you're alright . . .?

Zhenya   You'll have to go slowly, or I won't keep up.

Alright. Go on.

Lyuba   Wait, I have to think. So, this is the first page of the first chapter – 'Basic Histology'.

She begins to dictate the remembered text.

Histology of blood. Introduction. Blood consists of cells, both red cells and white cells, Erythrocytes and Leukocytes. Also, extracellular material . . . .

Zhenya   Wait, wait! I got as far as cells.

Lyuba   Red cells and white cells, Erythrocytes and Leukocytes.

Zhenya   . . . Leukocytes . . .

Lyuba   Also extracellular material . . . exceeding the volume of the cells. The total volume of blood in a mature adult is six litres . . . It is propelled through the cardiovascular system by means of the heart . . . Blood functions severally, including: the transportation of nutrients and the transportation of oxygen . . . also the removal of waste and carbon dioxide . . .

Hammering at the door. The women start.

Zhenya   Who's there?

No answer. **Lyuba** *goes to answer. It's* **Nikita**, *with a bundle of sticks.*

Lyuba   You, again.

Nikita   For the fire, Lyuba.

Lyuba *takes the sticks.*

Zhenya, *unnoticed, looks at her blood-stained handkerchief.*

Lights down.

Four

Yard. Morning. Offstage, sporadic hammering. **Nikita** *has a plank of wood in his hand. He is feeling the weight of it. Enter* **Dad**, *bringing a small pile of old planks, all with nails – and drops them in a heap.*

Dad   Pulling nails and pulling women – work of a lifetime.

Nikita   Like in the army. Getting wood's the easy part.

Filthy laugh from **Dad**, *slapping his son on the back.*

Dad   Ha! I knew it! He enlisted a boy and they made him a man.

Off you go.

He hands the pliers over, produces a bottle and settles to watch.

(*The sky.*) Not bad, between the rain.

So enlighten my wits, Nikit. What happens to a war vet after dark?

'When he comes back, if he comes back, I'll never be alone.'

I shouted your name last night. Guess what the walls said back? Save your breath, old man, he's pissed off again.

Nikita   I like to walk at night, clear my head.

Dad   Hour after hour, in darkness?

Beat.

Nikita   It's good we have all this. The foreman's kind.

Dad   Foreman's a fool. Thinks young hands about the place means prospects – the Revolution delivers. 'When the country needs new houses, we'll make new roofs.'

Till then, same old thing; drag out what's left, cut away the rot, make the best of it.

Nikita   Not such bad work

Dad   Not for the first ten years. Here – do what I do . . . imagine you're a dentist.

He pulls out the nail with a yank of the pliers.

Rotten. See? That's your tobacco, corporal.

Nikita *follows suit, holding up a nail/tooth.*

Nikita   Your vodka, Father.

Dad   Ha!

They toss the nails into a pile. Pause.

Dad   So, what d'you say this girl's name is?

Nikita   Ha! Nice try, Old Man.

Dad   Why be coy about it? In the old days we rolled in the hay one day, married the next.

The day I married your mother she could hardly walk up the aisle.

Time to pick the grass seeds out came later. Grass seeds, skin, then she got down to the bones – bloody woman never gave me five minutes – pick pick pick.

Odd what you miss.

Pretty, is she, this girl of yours?

Nikita   I said, I was walking last night.

Dad   And the night before?

Whoring, were you?

Nikita   Marching. That's the good part of it. Soldiering. One boot after the other. Simple.

Dad *shrugs.*

Dad   Today shows its bare arse to the past.

Next time you go to her, let me come, I'll check her out for you. Whores and horses, start with the teeth.

Nikita   Dad.

She's no whore.

Beat.

Dad   Oh God. It's not hers is it? This coffin?

Oh my stoopid mouth . . .!

Nikita   Lyuba's fine.

Dad   Thank Christ for that.

(*A penny drops.*) L-y-u-b-a . . . I knew it! Nikit's got a girl and her name is Lyuba. Who is she? You can tell me. What's her family?

Nikita   You won't remember.

Dad   I know them?

Nikita   The schoolteacher. She died a while back.

Dad   Peter and Paul. I remember her china.

If it's not for Lyuba what are you so po-faced about? Someone died, you got work – no sadness there.

Nikita   A friend of hers. She was alive till we met. Zhenya.

Dad   Oh ho, back five minutes and he knows two women!

Nikita   She was a good friend to Lyuba.

Now Lyuba's alone.

Dad   It was her you liked, was it – Zelda.

Nikita   Zhenya.

Dad   A looker, was she? You can tell me, I was a man before I was your dad.

Nikita   She took my hand.

If I'd met her first, if she'd ever been kind, who knows.

They say you can tell. Who'll make it, who won't.

It was rubbish in the war. Rubbish now.

Dad   Take my advice; if this Lyuba's not too plain to get you stiff, marry her now, while she's low. Not so many fellas around she can be choosy.

Nikita   The coffin has to be smooth, a good job. For Lyuba's sake.

Dad   Do what I showed you; let the eye lead the plane, the plane lead the hand. The other hand – that takes the cash, eh?

Pause, **Nikita** *lost in thought.*

Dad   Come on, I'll help. We've got this lot, we can borrow any tools, it'll be fine. Just . . .

Do one thing for me.

Nikita   ?

Dad   I should have found a woman myself. I don't mean for the chores, I can manage them. Someone to work around, complain about. Nag the pants off me morning till night.

I always meant to find someone, after your mother. You lose hope when you're old. Courage.

Let me hold you, Nikit, like I used to. Just for a moment.

Nikita   You held me when I came home.

Dad   Give up walking all night – bring this Lyuba home if you like, you can have my bed, I'll sleep in the narrow one. I won't listen.

Nikita   Not yet. I can't rush things.

Pause.

Dad   I know about war, Nikit.

All those hours lying in a field, faking wounds.

Things you did, things you didn't do. Your worst enemy gets blown to bits, you want to drag the bits together, make it right, like before.

Walk away. He would! The enemy, if he could. He'd lay you down, use yer back for a bridge, walk right over you.

Pick up where you left off, or start a new life.

Dare to fall asleep again, that's the real test.

Or keep moving. Eh? Marching.

Beat.

Nikita (*a confession*)   In the war, near the beginning . . .

Pause.

Dad   Son . . .?

Nikita *chooses the easier option. He stands. Holds out his arms.*

They embrace.

Dad   That's better.

Just you came home, Nikit.

You'll do.

Better half a worker than none, eh?

Dad, *tearful, makes to exit.*

Nikita   Where now? Not another drink?

Dad   Wood'll plane down well enough. You need new fastenings.

The foreman owes me. I brought him the future. The Revolution.

He exits.

Nikita *removes another nail and holds it to the light, examining its bent and twisted shape.*

He picks up a hammer and begins to tap the nail against a rock, straightening out the nail.

When he's satisfied, he holds it up again.

Nikita (*calling*)   These'll do fine.

Offstage, dogs bark. Bowing to his **Dad**'s *judgement,* **Nikita** *tosses the nail back on the pile, then sees . . .*

The **Tramp,** *carrying a bundle of belongings, crossing the stage, halts.*

Nikita *stands, and watches him.*

Nikita   You.

The **Tramp** *disappears.*

Nikita *sits down again, and begins yanking out the nails, distracting himself with work, glancing up to see if the* **Tramp** *is still there, then carrying on. Offstage, the hammering continues.*

Lights out.

Five

By the river, another cold day. **Lyuba** *and* **Nikita** *have been for a long walk and are now nearly home.* **Lyuba** *enters first, and stands on something – tiptoe, or a tree trunk.*

Lyuba   You can see my house from here. Looks almost new.

Pause.

You look serious.

Nikita   Yes.

Lyuba   You didn't always frown. You chased me round the garden once – while the grown-ups were talking – remember?

When you're young getting caught is the most thrilling bit. I didn't think to be quiet.

Smiles.

I should be sensible now. I have to go to work.

Nikita   I was wondering if we'll be married, Lyuba. Now we've got used to each other.

Beat.

Lyuba   Is this you asking me to be your wife?

Nikita (*formally*)   I would like you to be my wife, comrade.

Beat.

Lyuba   Alright. We could do it in the spring, after the exams. You can wait that long, can you? You won't die of passion?

Nikita   I'll wait.

Lyuba   I'm not such a tasty morsel. You only think I am. You're sure are you? I am still quite young, it'll be a long marriage.

Nikita   I'm sure.

Lyuba   Once my exams are over, we can register with the soviet. That's how it's done; people sign a book and it's legal, just like that. I'll be your bride, and you'll be my husband.

She wraps her arms around him, but he is awkward.

Nikita   How are your feet today?

Lyuba   My feet are fine. Aching.

These boots were good, once. Austrian. My mother's.

When I was really young I used to stand on a chair and watch down the inside of the piano while she played. The way the hammers bashed the wires. I used to feel so sorry for the wires, screaming out every time they were kicked.

Now the wires and my toes are just the same. Bash bash bash – all day long.

Nikita   I could rub them, if you like, your toes – then they won't hurt.

Lyuba   Not now. The pain will pass, I learned that from the hospital.

It usually blinks first, you just have to stare it down. Even pain has its breaking point.

Pause.

Lyuba   It was kind what you did for Zhenya, you and Mikhail.

Thank you.

Maybe the commander will get you some orders, now he knows how quickly you can work. What do you think?

Nikita   I think we should live together. I could come to your house.

Lyuba   No. If we're going to be married, you should stay at your house. When I'm qualified, we'll sort things out then, make decisions. We'll get married and be very ordinary; Lyuba and Nikita, comrades in marriage.

Nikita   I could be talking to you, keep the place warm . . .

Lyuba   After the exams. We'll talk then, make plans.

I still haven't decided how many children we'll have yet.

Your father might need one room I suppose – will he?

Mikhail?

Or we might live in some other place, miles from here.

Who knows what the future will be, once I've qualified.

The great thing is, nothing we'll do has been done before.

Tomorrow is another world.

I've made some decisions. Our first daughter will be called Zhenya, and our first son we'll call Nikit.

All our children will go to school and learn everything about the world downstream. And we'll be happy.

That's the only thing, Nikit, we mustn't be sad.

While I'm alive, while you're alive – that would be wrong.

We have each other to think of. So, no more sadness. Deal?

Nikita   Deal. If we live, we live for each other.

Lyuba   Stay by the river if you want to. Or go home.

We have to be strong for each other now, that's our real work.

She is leaving for work – and makes to exit.

Nikita   I saw the man again. The tramp.

Lyuba   The who?

Nikita   The tramp I followed. That's how I got home. I walked in his tracks, and the tracks led me here.

Lyuba   A tramp? He isn't here now though . . .?

Nikita *shrugs or shakes his head.*

Lyuba   No more tramp, Nikit. Go home. I'll come to see you later. Go on, take the good doctor's advice.

Nikita   You're not qualified.

Lyuba   Go!

Nikita   You first.

Lyuba   You.

Nikita   No, you.

Lyuba   You go.

Nikita *and* **Lyuba**   YOU.

Pause.

Lyuba   I have to work, Nikit. It's not just soldiers who live for other people. I have to qualify for Zhenya now. That comes first.

You understand, I know you do.

He does. She kisses the top of his head.

Nikita   They asked for volunteers, for the villages. Fixing school desks. I could join the work party. Keep my mind calm till the spring.

Lyuba   Perfect.

Nikita   We'll be gone a few weeks, I think.

Lyuba   Oh.

No, that's good. Volunteer, Nikit. We'll both work all the hours we can, and in the spring, we'll have our reward. Our life will begin.

She kisses him again on the top of his head.

I can't be late. I'll see you this evening.

She exits, and then calls.

Lyuba (*off*)   Go home, Nikit.

Nikita (*calling*)   Going.

A pause. The sound of a stick, snapping. **Nikita** *looks about him.*

Nikita   I know you're here.

I know that.

I'm fixed now. I'm healed.

Nothing appears. **Nikita** *exits in the opposite direction.*

Lights down.

Six

Lyuba's *house.* **Dad** *is offstage, calling.*

Dad   Anyone home?

Hello-o?

Dad *enters with a double wardrobe strapped to his back. He turns a full 360 degrees, but it's too heavy to play that game for long. He lets the wardrobe down carefully into the middle of the room.*

He looks around, goes to the fire, stokes it, glances about, lifts the kettle onto the stove. He settles into the chair.

Lyuba *returns from work.*

Lyuba (*off*)   Who's there? Is someone . . .

(*Startled, but recovering.*) Ah, Mikhail. It's you.

Dad   Lyuba.

A wedding gift. I copied your mother's furniture – the fretwork, I carved that from memory.

Lyuba *takes in the wardrobe – ugly enough to leave her speechless.*

Lyuba   I don't know what to say.

Dad   'Thank you' is traditional.

Lyuba   Thank you, father-in-law. It's kind of you.

Awkward pause.

Dad (*unimpressed*)   Nikit fixed the stool, then.

Lyuba *hangs up her coat.*

Lyuba   Yes. I saved some of the small things.

Dad   Seemed very grand this house, when I was here.

She was a handsome woman, your mother.

Too old for me, I told her.

Beat.

Lyuba   It's good of you to remember her. Thank you.

Pause. He clearly has no intention of going. She sees he has put the kettle on.

Lyuba   Can I make you a hot drink, papochka?

He nods. She sets about it, pouring at the stove. His half-jack of vodka is visible in his pocket as he looks around.

Dad   Did you hear anything from Nikit?

Lyuba   No – you?

He craftily swigs from the bottle.

Dad   Never around when you need him. That's how things are with Nikit – out of sight, out of mind.

Lyuba   He'll be busy. You know what that's like.

She gives him the drink.

Dad   You're made from sturdy stuff.

Lyuba   How's that?

Dad   You'll breed now, I suppose, the two of you.

Lyuba   We hope to have children. Why not?

Dad   Why not – the future needs lodgers as well as leaders.

Lyuba   Why shouldn't they be anything?

Dad   Nikit says you study all night.

Lyuba   For my exams. I study medicine.

Dad   You've grown into a fine woman, Lyuba. That's clear.

Lyuba   Thank you.

Dad   Can't be easy, with a boy like Nikit. He's a one-off, not a chip off the old block like we thought.

Leaving you alone week after week, night after night.

Lyuba   You forget – I'm used to being alone. Like you.

Dad   Different for you lot, I suppose.

Lyuba   Me and Nikita?

Dad   This generation. We knew the present was all we had; didn't fritter youth away being sensible. (*Scoffing.*) The future.

We had living to do. Flesh and blood. People lived like there was no tomorrow when I was young.

Lyuba   Times change, papochka. The world is different now.

Dad   Not people. Men and women. We're still creatures, underneath, rutting in season, out of season, why not?

Pause. We're getting into a weird area here.

Lyuba   Drink your coffee, papochka.

Dad   It's a bit hot, just yet.

Lyuba   Drink up – and go home.

Beat.

Dad   You're wasting the best time of your life, Lyuba . . .

Lyuba   Drink, papochka. If you would.

She has quietly armed herself with a frying pan.

He hesitates, then accepts her rejection, exasperated.

Dad   Sod it. Let me know when you're ready for this wedding, not a church one I imagine? Figures. I'll fetch Nikit back, when you're . . . (ready).

Lyuba   My exams are over now, almost – you can fetch Nikita home anytime you like. Thank you.

Dad   If you're sure that's what's what you want.

She is implacable. He raps on the side of the wardrobe.

Dad   Nikit, get back here. Nikit!

Magically, **Nikita** *appears –* **Dad** *covers his nose with a handkerchief.*

Nikita   Dad!

Dad   Dear Christ. Did you wash since you left?

Nikita   Everything is smoke and dust out there – and sickness. They take up trees to make the pyres. The soil blows all over.

Dad   You're in luck – Lyuba's all yours apparently. Go on, get the pair of you wed.

Nikita   She's ready for me?

Dad (*sotto*)   Take my advice, she's like a bitch on heat.

Nikita *and* **Lyuba** *are alone, though* **Dad** *is still onstage.*

Lyuba   Nikita.

Nikita *produces pots of flowers.*

Nikita   A wedding gift, from the workers. They're jealous – of me, of us, marrying for love. I'm the luckiest man in the world.

Lyuba   The women at the hospital say the same; Lucky Lyuba.

Nikita   The now and future man.

Lyuba   They're right, they're right to be jealous.

Pregnant pause.

Lyuba   So, this is now, husband. Finally.

Beat. **Dad** *clears his throat, smacks his lips – hands back his mug.*

Dad   I'll be off then.

He embraces **Nikita***, then bows his head formally to* **Lyuba***.*

Dad   Good luck to you both.

(*Sotto.*) Before . . . I just get lonely, Ly / uba . . .

Lyuba   Goodbye, papochka.

Nikita   What's that?

Dad *and* **Lyuba**   Nothing.

Lyuba   Papa's going.

Nikita   Thank you. For the furniture.

Dad   The walls and me, we know each other's ways. They don't bother me, I don't bother them. Even the mirror doesn't look at you twice when you're old.

You know where I am.

He exits. The young couple are alone.

Lyuba   I've cooked some supper, if you want it.

Nikita   I've got another gift.

He opens the wardrobe and passes out an unfeasible number of small chairs, painted red.

Nikita   For the children.

Lyuba   You made them?

Nikita   The paint's dry now, almost.

Lyuba   They're wonderful!

Where will I put them – here?

Or here?

Nikita   And a table, we'll need that for them too . . .

. . . and this is for you. So you'll be warm in winter.

Lyuba   Your coat – you shouldn't have cut your coat!

Nikita   I have this jacket of Dad's. I'll be fine, knowing you're warm. Wrapped up from the cold.

Lyuba   Too thick for now.

A moment as they gaze at the little scene – several small chairs around a small table.

Lyuba   I have nothing to give you.

Beat. She puts the coat down.

Will we go to bed now, husband?

He nods. Sensing his sudden uncertainty – and taking it for nerves – she kisses him.

Lyuba   Who needs a church wedding? We're each other's. By law.

She presses herself against him, kissing him again – but he breaks away.

Nikita   Wait.

Lyuba   Nikita?

Nikita   My heart hurts.

Pause.

Lyuba   Will I undress for you, Nikita Firsov?

*She takes his long glance as one of desperate want. She begins to undress, self-conscious but excited. After a moment or two, **Nikita** crosses quietly to the wardrobe and begins to undress behind it, getting down to his longjohns. Then he stops, listening, almost afraid to come out from his hiding place. She stops undressing. She is on the verge of humiliation.*

Lyuba   Is this how we're going to live, so ashamed of ourselves?

Nikita   I don't know why you love me, Lyuba.

Lyuba   Because I can. Despite everything, we can love.

Pause.

This is strange.

Nikita *emerges.*

Nikita   In the village . . . I don't know if I was awake but . . . I saw us, up there – in the ceiling, between the rafters . . . you were there, we were together, two flies, bound up . . . are they alive, dead? . . . I couldn't tell. I had no idea. I couldn't tell.

What are we, Lyuba?

Lyuba   We're not that are we – flies?

Beat.

Nikita, did you get hurt, in the war? You should tell me, if it's bad, I can help . . .

Nikita   I was hurt. I healed.

She feels his forehead.

Lyuba   You have a temperature.

She gets a grip of herself.

Forget wedding nights. What does it matter . . .?

I'm Lyuba Firsova. We've got a whole life ahead of us. And a life can be full of so much – work, and food, and caring – seasons pass, years will pass . . .

She tenderly straightens his hair, then playfully opens the door of the wardrobe.

We have a wardrobe, bigger than some people's houses – ugly, but its ours.

We have furniture – for very small guests.

We have everything. Enough for some kind of future? Don't we?

He nods, uncertainly.

Lyuba   Give me your hands.

Zhenya was right, your lifeline goes on for ever.

Nikita   ?

Lyuba   You're a good man, Nikita. And one day soon, when you're well, when you've gone off me a bit, your old strength will come back. The strength we had when we ran round the yard. We'll be happy.

She kisses his hands.

If we can't lie together, if it's too painful for you now, we can stand. Like this. For ever.

Nikita   Just stand?

Lyuba   Just here.

She kisses his hand and rests her head on his chest – then pulls back.

You're hot. Feverish.

Stay there.

He coughs.

She folds back the bed clothes.

Get in the bed. Keep your clothes on, we have to keep you warm.

Pause as she looks at him.

Get into bed, Nikit.

Get in the . . .

Get in the bed!

GET IN THE BED!

Agggghhhhh!

She steps toward him as if to strike him – sheer frustration – but before she is anywhere close, **Nikita** *collapses on the floor.*

Beat.

Lyuba   Oh God.

She is so fearful – she's been here before, with her mother.

She goes to the door and looks out, as if thinking of going or calling for help. She changes her mind, or perhaps there's no one to ask.

She closes the door/turns back in. She has chosen to stay inside with him.

I was trained for this. Every day I go to work, and I tend people – comrades.

You have to be kept warm.

Stove.

She adjusts the stove.

She goes to him and takes him under the armpits and tries to move him. Impossible.

She tries again. She manages to shift him towards the bed a little. She drags him further – he's a dead weight, exhausting. She keeps on.

She gets him onto the bed, or near it, and pulls the bedclothes on him. She fetches his coat and piles that on top too.

She wonders what else to do. She is cold herself. She looks towards the yard, and starts to make a joke, which dies on her lips.

You can't die, Nikit. Who'll make the casket . . .?

*She looks at **Nikita**.*

*She takes off her shoes, lies beside **Nikita**, folds herself round him. His teeth are chattering.*

Lyuba   That's what the flies were doing – surviving. You see.

Sssshhh. Take my warmth.

Ssssh.

Lights down.

Seven

*Lights up in **Lyuba**'s house, some days later. The bed is empty. The door is kicked open from outside. **Nikita** enters, carrying a bucket of mud. He sits at the little table, a pile of clay already on it. He is fashioning it into a mountain, but strange and misshapen. He is lost in his work.*

Lyuba *enters, wrapped in her coat, as if she has come home from work.*

Nikita *barely looks up.*

Lyuba   You're up. Third day running, that's good.

Nikita   I'm fine. Stronger.

Pause.

She flops straight down on the bed, and lies back, kicks her shoes off, exhausted.

Nikita *sits back from his work, and studies it.*

Nikita   Could be a mountain, I think. (*More certainly.*) A mountain.

Lyuba   What's that sticking out? At the side?

Nikita   Which side?

Lyuba   There.

He shrugs, they consider it, and then he mashes it up again.

Lyuba   Oh don't do that – I could have worked it out.

Nikita   It's just a . . . thing.

Lyuba   If it means something it can be worked out, can't it? Understood.

Looked like an ear, the sticky-out part.

Nikita   The ear of a mountain . . .

Lyuba   Why not. The river babbles doesn't it? 'The mouth of the river'?

Foot of the mountain.

Nikita   Shoulder of the hill.

Lyuba   Brow of the hill.

Nikita   Bottom of the pit.

Smiles.

Lyuba   I like it when you make things. Make the tree again, with the tangled roots. That was scary – I had nightmares after that.

She hangs up her coat.

Is that what you've done today? Made your worlds?

Nikita   I did the cleaning, I cut some wood.

Lyuba   Made worlds.

Nikita   The army had a shipment come in. Coffins, hundreds. Nobody needs new houses. Nobody needs new furniture. They inherit it, or just take it from an empty house.

Lyuba   Or have it thrust on them by relatives.

Give me your hand.

He moves to sit by the bed and she puts his hand on her belly.

Nikita   What's this?

Lyuba   It's nothing. Nothing at all.

Beat. **Nikita** *withdraws his hand.*

Lyuba   Do you want beer tonight?

Nikita   No. Thanks.

Lyuba   It was cold last night. I was cold.

Nikita   I kept you awake, did I?

Lyuba   Shouting? A little. Then going out.

Nikita   What did I say?

Lyuba   It's not just rivers that babble. Just the same old thing. All the lovers you had before you met me.

Nikita   Ha!

Pause.

Lyuba   Let's get the bed near the stove tonight.

Come on. Leave that now.

They push the bed centre stage, shift the table, etc.

Lyuba   I want to be roasting tonight. I'm not going to take a stitch off. If I sweat like a donkey and I stink in the morning I don't care.

Nikita   Lovely.

Lyuba   See? It's so much warmer. We don't waste the fire, and we can stretch out as much as we like.

She lies down on the bed – a clear invitation.

Nikita   I'll . . . go for a piss.

You want to eat?

Lyuba   No. There was bread at the hospital.

He exits to the washroom.

Lyuba (*half-calling*)   I lay awake all night last night, truthfully.

Did you hear the dogs bark when someone passed by? I was thinking about Alexei, this boy at the hospital. Little Alexei.

We lost him today. He wasn't dead then, last night.
Last night there was hope, that's what kept me awake I think. The cells, buzzing under the microscope.

He doesn't need a casket; I asked but they're rich. *Were* rich, before the war. The mother, when she came in, after the boy died, she wasn't rich then, she was so – blank. Not angry, not shouting, like rich people do. Blank. Like someone turned a tap off.

He slipped away just as the sun came out, and I thought, what horrible timing. He missed all this.

Like that time we lay on the ice, do you remember? We saw the river running underneath us and you said – lucky river!

The water's here, just like us, but soon it'll be flowing past fresh flowers and new grass, and all the way out to the sea.

She begins to sing – a lilting melody.

At length, **Nikita** *enters from the washroom, and stands, listening.*

He joins in tentatively at first, then he starts to push the pace, turning it almost into a roistering drinking song. They end laughing.

Lyuba   Come on, into bed.

She slaps the bed next to her.

He gets in, lies flat on his back, she gropes him. He pushes her off. Unfazed, she throws her arm across him, nuzzling up, smiling.

A pause.

Nikita   It's hot.

He moves her arm away.

Lyuba   Your fever's gone. You fought the infection. You survived.

Nikita Firsov: the man who wouldn't die.

She lies waiting for something to happen.

He gets up and picks up the kerosene lamp.

Nikita   Should I put the light out?

Lyuba   If you like. If that's what you want.

He just stands there. **Lyuba** *tries to keep her voice steady.*

Lyuba   You're my husband, Nikit. I'm your wife.

He doesn't respond. **Lyuba** *rolls over, away from him, curling up in a ball.*

Nikita *makes to exit.* **Lyuba** *speaks in the darkness.*

Lyuba   Do you think it helps, walking away?

Nikita   I'm just walking.

Lyuba   Are you?

The door closes. **Nikita** *walks, and walks straight into . . .*

Eight

A sharp morning. Downstage, by the frozen river.

Birdsong.

The **Tramp** *is spreading the ashes of his fire.*

Nikita *enters from upstage and, seeing him, strikes up a very one-sided conversation.*

Nikita   Even the birds are starving round here. That's why they sing – for their supper.

(*Yelling at them.*) Banshees!

Strangers will come fishing soon, from the town. Once the ice melts. Men, boys. You know it's spring when boys come with hooks and clubs, to kill things. They have to eat too, I suppose.

The **Tramp** *ignores him.*

Nikita   When spring does come, when the ice breaks, I'll take my chance, drown myself. That'll be best. If you saw the way Lyuba looks at me – Lyuba, that's my wife, my comrade, the woman I . . . (love).

The **Tramp** *has picked up a rock, and passes it to* **Nikita** *– go ahead. The* **Tramp** *goes back to his preparations.* **Nikita** *looks at the rock and the ice on the river.*

Nikita   Why not. I'm holding up the future.

The **Tramp** *makes to exit.*

Nikita   Do you have some kind of plan? Do you know where the path leads? Or do you just follow, like some bloody idiot?

The **Tramp** *exits.* **Nikita** *hesitates, then sees the* **Tramp***'s bundle.*

Nikita   Wait, you've left . . .

He drops the rock, picks up the bag . . . then decides to look inside.

Nikita *slowly pulls out a severed head.*

He stares at it, then lowers it back into the sack.

Alright.

Yes.

He puts the sack down, heaves the rock into the river. We hear the ice break with a crash.

He picks up the sack and exits, following the **Tramp***.*

Lights down.

Silence.

The stumbling piano music returns.

End of Part One – Interval.

Part Two

Nine

Lights up: winter, in a new, open space, littered with a few cabbage leaves.

Downstage, a tarpaulin over a mound of rubbish.

Offstage, the voice of a **Market Trader**. *He monotonously calls out his offer.*

Market Trader (*off*)   Two for fifty, four for ninety, or whatchyagot.

This is repeated endlessly, monotonously.

Market Trader (*off*)   Two for fifty, four for ninety, or whatchyagot.

While this is going on, upstage, with his back to us, hat pulled low, a man sweeps. He turns at length and sweeps his way downstage to centre stage. This is **Vlass**. *As he gets there,* **Paulina** *enters with a bowl of watery peelings, stage left. She walks centre stage and maliciously tips the peelings at his feet.*

She turns on her heels and goes to exit the way she came.

Market Trader (*off*)   Two for fifty, four for ninety, or whatchyagot.

Vlass   Wassat for! What now?

Paulina   Tell that moron to shut it!

She exits.

Market Trader (*off*)   Two for fifty, four for ninety, or whatchyagot.

Vlass (*calling after her*)   Issa market day!

Market Trader (*off*)   Two for fifty, four for ninety, or whatchyagot.

(*Off.*) Two for fifty, four for ninety, or whatchyagot.

Vlass   Arkady – give it a rest, comrade.

Market Trader (*off*)   Two for . . .

Vlass   Enough!

Silence. **Vlass** *carries on sweeping.*

Paulina *enters again, with a package of peelings this time.*

Vlass   Happy?

Paulina (*mimicking*)   'Two for fifty, four for ninety or whatchyagot' – like bees in my head, all day, 'Two for fifty, four for ninety . . .' (*Calling.*) Change the tune, can't yer?!

Vlass (*remonstrating*)   He's stopped!

She continues to the tarp and pulls back the corner, intending to dump the rubbish.

Paulina   Oh yeah, *now* he has, *now* he's stopped. What about before, what about all morning? 'Two for fifty, four for . . .'

Aaagh!

Underneath the tarp, the **Tramp**; *a human being – just – dressed in black, head wrapped in a scrap of old blanket, curled up, keeping out the cold.* **Paulina** *screams again, more deliberately this time. It fails to have the desired effect on* **Vlass**, *who laughs.*

She calms herself.

Paulina   You are doing this on purpose. You are supposed to be the supervisor. Get rid of it!

Vlass   Rid of what?

Paulina   The tramp.

Vlass   Again?

He approaches the figure to look, and pokes it with the broom handle.

Vlass   Oy!

What is it, deaf? Or snuffed it.

Paulina   Get rid.

She leaves him to it.

Vlass   Oy . . .

She is gone. **Vlass** *addresses the* **Tramp***.*

Vlass   Oy. You.

Not *that* cold last night. Go on, get out of it.

No movement. He sighs. He checks the coast is clear, then starts to make a roll-up.

What language is it you don't speak, then? Some foreign crap, no point wastin' on us peasants?

Can't say I blame yer.

Me? I'm dumb in all the major tongues.

My wife, on the other hand, my wife's a reg'lar professor. Oh yeah. She'll give you a right lesson, she get's hold of you.

Enter **Paulina***, with a bucket of grim-looking slops. She pours them luxuriantly over the* **Tramp** *and exits.*

Beat.

Vlass   Told yer.

The figure reacts, unhurriedly. It shakes itself off, moves a few feet away, to a dry spot, and lies down again. **Vlass** *watches all this.*

Vlass   See, a deaf man wouldn't do that.

Even a deaf-head knows what's coming, spares himself.

You're a right pain in the arse.

Not deaf, but *def*-initely in the way. Go on, get out of it, 'fore I have to make you. Shift it. Now.

The figure doesn't respond.

Vlass *sighs again. He reluctantly puts down the broom and picks up a length of heavier wood, feels its weight like a baseball bat, approaches the figure and belts the man viciously in the midriff. The* **Tramp** *creases in pain, but makes no sound. He staggers up onto all fours.*

Vlass   Not completely senseless then. Go on, piss off.

Tramp *moves a short way away, and lies down again.*

This is now a serious challenge.

Vlass *walks over to the figure, and positions himself, winding up a big one.*

Vlass   I'll count to three, you bag of shit. Alright?

One!

He brings the club crashing into the figure's ribs. Again the figure makes no sound, but curls into a tight ball.

Two!

Again he brings the club into the figure's ribs. And again . . .

Three!

He casts an anxious glance in the direction of his wife.

Had enough? I have. I'm knackered.

Go on, do us both a favour, clear off.

The figure slowly, very painfully, gets to his feet moves a few feet away, and lies down again.

Vlass   Jesus Christ, Peter and Paul – deaf, dumb and stupid.

Oy!

He swings a kick at the **Tramp**'*s head – then sees the* **Tramp** *has got a bag.*

Vlass   Oy oy, watchyagot there?

Market Trader (*off*)   Two for fifty, four for ninety, or watchya . . .

Vlass (*calling*)   Shut it!

Give it here. Give it.

He glances around, then prises the bag away from the semi-conscious man, who resists.

Vlass   Oh, got some energy now 'ave yer.

He gets the bag, feels the weight of whatever's inside, and gingerly pulls out . . . a rotten cabbage.

Oh God, how long you 'ad that in there?

He tosses the cabbage away, appalled by the stench, and tips out the sack. Two small clinking things land on the floor – he picks up first one, then the other. Holds them up to the light.

What's this – Horse? A dog?

The other figure is human-shaped.

Times are hard, comrade, no market for toys. A real horse, folks can eat. A real dog folks'll eat . . . A real man . . . I don't listen to rumours.

He chucks the bag down then, relenting, picks up a few scraps – cabbage leaves, other rubbish – and puts it in the bag.

Look take this, and this, and go somewhere else, alright? 'fore I have to sweep you there in bits.

*He offers the bag to the **Tramp**, who doesn't move. **Vlass** gives up.*

Vlass   You know what I think? God made the world in six days.

On the seventh he says, 'Oy Comrade Lenin – take the world apart in five years, an' it's all yours.'

Geddit?

No.

He glances around himself, nervously; who knows who might be listening?

Don't make much sense to me, neither.

He stares at the prone figure. He sniffs, looks about him, back to the figure. Thinks. He yells offstage.

Vlass   Oy. OY, Paulina!

Come and give us a hand.

We got lucky.

Enter **Paulina***, talking as she comes.*

Paulina   What you talkin' about – luck(y)? Oh Christ, what's that? I told you to get rid. What you want to save it for?

Vlass   Bring a chair.

Paulina   A chair?

Vlass   A stool then.

He pulls the dead weight upright, while **Paulina** *brings the stool. Between them they prop him up.* **Vlass** *pulls off the* **Tramp***'s hat or hood.*

We now see it is **Nikita***, bloodied and badly beaten – what we've just witnessed is only the latest beating.*

Paulina   Christ. What you done now?

You've let the cat right out of the bag.

Vlass   ?

Paulina   You shouldn't do it, I told yer.

Vlass   Do what?

Paulina   Beat 'em up. You ain't strong enough. Get the others on it. I only said shift him, get someone else t'do the proper work.

You're the supervisor not a watchman. Look at your beard.

Grey as a fucking leper these days.

Vlass   What?

Paulina   Your beard, grey as a leper.

Vlass   Grey as a . . .?

Pepper. The phrase is, grey as a . . .

(*Emphatic, exasperated, correcting himself.*) Grey as pepper.

Paulina   That's what I'm saying. Take care of yourself once in a while. Recognise your station. Take care of me once in a while wouldn't go amiss.

Vlass   You? Put horse shit in the barrer once in a while might be a start.

Paulina   I do my share and you know it.

Vlass   Oh yeah.

Paulina   You should pass the work on, I'm tellin' yer.

Vlass   What? I've always got one or two of 'em set on. Not my fault they piss off, soon as fed.

Paulina   You don't beat 'em 'ard enough, that's the trouble.

Vlass   You don't feed 'em well enough.

Paulina   I don't get the ingredients.

Vlass   What are you talking about, ingredients, you live in a bloody market! You ain't starvin'.

Paulina   Get rid of him. He stinks. Makes my skin crawl jus' lookin' at 'im.

Vlass   Soon. A comrade can give a comrade a smoke if he wants, can't he?

He pushes a cigarette between **Nikita**'s *busted lips.*

Paulina   Oh Christ, not another one.

Vlass   What?

Paulina   Beggars, tramps, all that sort – old soldiers. Stop picking them up. One after the other. I told yer, if it falls out the nest, let it die.

Vlass   What if he's not a tramp.

Paulina   Not a tramp . . .?! Look at it!

Vlass   He's an artist. Maybe. Toymaker.

Paulina   What you on about toymaker? You gone soft in the 'ead . . .

Vlass   This.

He passes **Paulina** *the bag. She opens it, recoils from the stench.*

Paulina   Christ! What died in here?

Vlass   Go on. Look.

She gingerly retrieves the figures and holds them to the light.

Paulina   Can't tell what that is . . . S'got legs . . . a dog?

Could be religious. Get rid.

Vlass   A religious dog?

Paulina   We could get implicated. Informed on.

You wanna face the rifles?

Nikita *smiles to himself.*

Paulina   Now look! You got him gibberring an' drooling, leaking out all over the place . . .

Nikita's *amusement sparks a coughing fit. He spits out blood onto the floor.*

Beat. **Paulina** *viciously clips him over the head.*

Vlass   Hey hey.

Paulina   Treat 'em like people, they behave like dogs. Who'd's he think he is, gettin' hisself beaten up? Spewing his filth on my ground?

Vlass   Soup. Fetch him some of that soup.

Paulina   What's this, officers' mess?

Vlass   Now!

Beat. Exit **Paulina**, *under sufferance.*

Vlass   What's your name then, Comrade Stupid Bugger? Mmm?

No words, no thoughts? Mind like a cave?

You'll get on well here.

(*Calling.*) This week's soup – alright?

Pause, while they smoke.

You may be in luck, as it 'appens.

You want peace and quiet, I can help.

What you like with latrines?

Latrine duty?

Musta done that in the army. Whatever else you are, she's right, gotta be a soldier.

First thing I learned when it was my turn: best to curl up for a kicking.

Then I learned latrine duty.

You prob'ly think I give a shit.

Red, White, bagman, thass your business, jus' do the work, and keep schtum about anything else you see round here.

Alright?

Nikita *meets his gaze.* **Vlass** *calculates.*

Vlass   Don't move.

He exits.

Pause. **Nikita** *probes his wounds.*

Vlass *returns with a shovel, and puts it into* **Nikita**'s *hand.*

Vlass   Here.

Nikita *doesn't so much take the spade as experiences it, the feel of it in his hand.*

Vlass   Ha! Like the thought of work, do yer? Maybe you're not a soldier, after all.

Paulina *returns with a bowl of soup.*

Paulina   This is it – last I got. I can't keep feeding 'em, they'll eat me out of house an' home.

Wassgoing on?

Vlass   Keep it. He'll want it after.

Paulina   After what?

Vlass   Go on, get on with it. Latrine's over there. 'Fore the light's gone.

Paulina   You never set him on . . .?! You never give him work?!

Nikita *gets up very stiffly, and nods, grateful for the job, then exits.*

Vlass (*calling after him*)   There's some lime back of the shed. And mind you do it proper; I want to eat my dinner off that latrine.

Paulina   Vlass Ivanovitch, you are unbelievable. Bleeding state of it!

Vlass   We'll see. One ear works at least – he can listen out for trouble.

Paulina   You're going soft.

Vlass   More use than you anyway.

Paulina   Oh great, thank you. All the years I give you?

Vlass   You want me to save my beard. I'm saving my beard.

What more do you want?!

Talk about bees in the head!

He exits, stormily. **Paulina**, *alone, speaks to herself.*

Paulina   What do I want?

What does any woman want.

Don't get me started, Vlass Ivanovitch,

I start on what I want, there won't be no end to it.

She drops the cloth onto the floor, and begins to wipe it. Lights.

Ten

Nikita *enters with a bloodstained butcher's block on wheels – a new day. He wears a smart new apron or other work gear. He sets about scrubbing the block. Blood runs up* **Nikita**'s *arms as he scrubs the block. He is now in much better shape, but still taciturn.*

Paulina *enters with a bucket and stands watching him.*

Paulina   Look at you, all strong and silent. No wastin' words with you, is there.

No response. She tries again.

Bad luck for toymakers; no kids round here.

Thass no surprise – me plumbing's wrecked, life I've had.

God knows how many little bastards he's got running around. Collects debts once a week.

Thass what he calls it.

She sits to peel vegetables into the bucket

Don't come near me no more. No honey in the pot, no use poking round in there. No one's got a spoon long enough for what's wrong with me.

I don't mind. Better off without. He's like a big kid hisself.

Good job we got someone round the place makes hisself useful, eh Croak?

Croak?

Nikita *does not respond.*

Paulina   Please yerself. You know me; not much fer conversation.

Pause.

You remind me of my first sweetheart, my friend's dad. He didn't talk much.

I got my first dose of crabs off of him.

Or one of his mates.

She scratches herself. Noises off – **Vlass** *is talking to someone.*

Vlass (*off*)   Ah, comrade – it's you again!

Paulina   Always someone getting under yer feet in this place.

Why can't they doss down somewhere else?

Everyone knows we have to keep the place tidy for the traders. Him getting the brewing going again, thass where the trouble is. Least you won't say nothing. You won't breathe a word about his hooch, will you, eh Croak?

Pause – again, he is not responding. She snaps.

Alright. Thass it.

She throws down the veg, wipes off the knife, takes out a bottle.

Paulina   You've been avoiding this fer days, don't think I don't know.

So what we up to? 'S'. We done S; T.

(*Thinks.*) Tomas. Taras? Tymor. Don't look like a Tymor Timofey? Younger. You a Timofeyavitch?

Oh go on, give us a clue for God's sake, we can't call you Croak for ever.

'Where's Croak?', 'You seen ol' Croak?'

'Croak fixed that stall up yet?'

Never thought you'd hold out this long, we nearly run out the alphabet.

Not Tihan . . . U's then . . . Ullrich.

No reaction.

No, alright then, how about V? Vladimir.

Nikita *glares at her.*

Paulina   Vassili? For the love of God give us a clue, you'll drive me mental, I was convinced you was a Ivan all last week, then I thought, 'What, Ivan, the soldier?' Bit obvious.

Don't think I could fancy another Ivan. Not after Vlass Ivanovitch.

You're not an Ivan are you? Croaky? Croak?

No response.

Getting worse, you are.

Suppose you could've forgot your name . . .

Who you are . . . Where you from . . .

Most of my life's best forgot.

I wouldn't've minded a few kiddies. We give it a good old go Vlass and me, at the start, my God we did.

Nothing works, thass the truth. Like a field of stones. All broke up, and no fixes.

Pause.

Nikita   Broke . . . Fix . . .

Paulina   What?

What d'you say?

Nikita   Broke, fix, clean, mend, listen, make, make . . . walk, eat, November – hungry, fucking – not fucking . . .

sing, animals, fur . . . ice, summer, river . . . rivering . . .
bobbing.

He runs out of words, and stands swaying a little.

Paulina (*concerned*)   Go on, Croaky. Don't stop. S'only me.

Say something more if you want – iss only me can hear yer.

Nikita *comes to, sees* **Paulina***, and goes back to scrubbing.*

Paulina   Suit yerself.

Thass not a clue is it? Scrubber?

She thinks this is hilarious.

Paulina   Hey, Vlass, I cracked it, iss not Croak, iss Scrubber!

Enter **Vlass**.

Vlass   Militia.

Paulina *reacts without missing a beat, dumping her bottle in the
peelings bucket, as the* **Investigator** *enters, wearing a worker's
jacket and cap.* **Vlass** *pulls a similar – but less impressive – cap
from somewhere and falls in line.* **Paulina***, acting her part, tears a
strip off* **Nikita***.*

Paulina   For the last time, I don't allow no illegal alcohol in
the bucket.

Market!

Oh. How can we be of service, Comrade Investigator? Cold
day, don't yer think?

Pause. **Investigator** *surveys the scene.*

Investigator   Well?

Vlass *indicates* **Nikita***.*

Vlass   Iss the only stranger we've seen, comrade.

Investigator   Alright. Bring him in.

Paulina   What you doing? You leave him alone, d'you hear, he's as good as gold, he is.

Vlass   Don't hinder the work of the militia, my love!

Paulina   Don't you 'my love' me! Comrade aren't I, same as you.

Investigator   The stranger is accused of theft. From the Party.

Paulina   Theft? Theft of what?

Vlass   Tools – from the agricultural collective.

Beat. **Paulina** *hides the paring knife behind her back.*

Paulina   Croak – after all we done for you? A common thief!

She slaps **Nikita**'s *face. The* **Investigator** *is unimpressed with this pantomime.*

Investigator   Clear the stalls.

Bring my equipment.

Paulina *and* **Vlass** *clear stage as prison cell is flown in, spinning as it comes. As it lowers,* **Vlass** *locks* **Nikita** *in the cell. A gramophone appears. Meanwhile, the* **Investigator** *takes out a record from its sleeve and places it on the gramophone.*

Vlass   Comrade Investigator, if I could have a word about the stranger . . .

Investigator   Hush, comrade. One moment.

The gramophone is wound up, the needle is dropped onto the record.

The court will pause for a moment of beauty.

Music plays – aria from Verdi's Rigoletto. *Finally it reaches its sublime end.*

Investigator   Well?

Vlass   Very nice, comrade.

Investigator   Lucky you weren't with us in the villages this week. If you care for beauty, it would have poisoned your ears.

Vlass   I was busy here, Comrade Investigator, keeping order in the market.

Investigator   Ha – not quite.

Life out there is worse than you can imagine.

A poet would struggle for words.

Orphans being hunted for food.

Imagine.

Try burying a corpse in some of those places, they'll shoot you with their last bullet. I know, I was shot at.

Don't put that corpse in the ground, this woman says to me; a land-owning woman, rich enough to own a gun.

That, there, is the body of my neighbour.

Oh, so you knew this man. Were you friendly with him?

No, says she, I hated him – but his flesh would feed my grandchildren for a week. Put that body in the ground, and you take the food right out of their mouths.

I mean it, she says, I'll shoot.

Then she shot.

Not a good shot, obviously.

Do you know where I got this gramophone?

Vlass   I have no idea, comrade.

Investigator   From the house of a very rich man, in the war.

When I woke in that village, last week – the day after we hung the woman with the gun – I thought, when I get out of this place, when I get back to town, to my office, the first thing I'm going to destroy is that recording. Beauty is obscene, in this circumstance. An affront to the way we live.

Vlass   I agree, Comrade Investigator.

Investigator   You do?

Vlass   I . . . we . . . reject all bourgeois entertainment.
Destroy the gramophone and the recording.

Investigator   Ha! But the gramophone is innocent. It only
plays what I give it.

Vlass   Then we should destroy the recording, comrade.

Investigator   But without the gramophone, it says nothing.
What we hear in this music, comrade, is the howl of a dying
world.

It was a harsh world for the likes of us, before the Revolution,
it was our lot to suffer then – now it's their turn: rich women,
landowners, artists.

Let them suffer, that's fair, but I wonder if the world we're
building will ever produce such a beautiful howl.

What do you think?

Pause. **Vlass** *is stuck for the correct words*.

Investigator   As I thought; you don't think.

So, what have we discovered concerning the present case?
This creature you've imprisoned.

Vlass   You said he stole tools from the agricultural
collective. Comrade.

Investigator   Does he admit the crime?

Vlass   He doesn't speak.

Investigator   A word of advice, comrade. Eyes and ears –
these are *our* tools. What's that, lying in the corner of the cell?

Vlass   Bread. He sometimes refuses to eat.

Investigator   Your conclusion?

Vlass   It could be . . . sabotage. He sabotages his life, and so betrays the Revolution.

Pause.

Investigator   Can you hear me, prisoner?

Vlass   It's possible he doesn't hear.

Investigator   He may not listen, that's different.

(*To* **Nikita**.) You. That's right.

What's to be said in your defence, comrade, mmm?

Silence.

Nothing. Throw him some bread.

Vlass *does so, throwing it as if to a duck.* **Nikita** *makes no move.*

The **Investigator** *passes over the charge sheet.*

Investigator   Read out the formal charge.

Vlass *reads, with effort.*

Vlass   Stealing of goods from the agricultural cooperative.

Sabotaging the progress of agricultural development.

Preventing the conveying of grain to relieve the cities.

A clear act of sabotage, which is in simple terms, treason. The forfeit is . . . death.

Investigator   Witnesses?

Vlass (*waving the charge sheet*)   The agricultural workers . . .

(*An idea.*) My wife has been watching him – she can vouch for him, comrade.

Investigator   Ha! Really. Bring her in.

Vlass (*calling off*)   In here, comrade. Now.

Paulina *enters.*

Investigator   Your worker is charged with theft from the agricultural cooperative. What do you say?

Paulina   Him? He's never been nowhere near cooperative, has he, Vlass?

Investigator   I also found him unresponsive to beauty. Did you notice that while he was in your care? Or perhaps the opportunity did not present itself.

Vlass   We could sing a patriotic song, Comrade Investigator.

Beat.

If he's innocent, the prisoner will respond.

Paulina   Good idea.

Investigator   Well, we've tried beauty, we may as well try bedlam.

Please.

Vlass   Me? Right . . .

He sings a patriotic song; **Paulina** *and* **Investigator** *dutifully join in. The song ends triumphantly. A pause.*

Investigator   Not a sound. Your conclusion?

Vlass   The prisoner refuses to do what's good for him.

Investigator   He refuses to sing, certainly.

Paulina   He only just started talking.

Investigator *and* **Vlass**   What?

Investigator   You questioned him already?

Paulina   All the time. Still don't know his name. Where he's from.

What he is. He just shows up one day. He's a good worker!

For an alien. And he's got thinner. Like you can see straight through him. Don't matter how much I feed him.

Investigator   Well, then. If there is no evidence for the defence . . .

He produces his pistol.

Paulina   . . . and he makes toys, don't he Vlass.

Investigator   Toys? Show me.

Vlass *produces the figure of a man from his pocket.*

Vlass   It's a man. There's a horse too, or a dog.

Paulina   It's not religious.

Investigator   Farm wire. Evidence.

What this man is doing in this town is stealing agricultural equipment at every opportunity. That is an act against the state.

Vlass   Allegedly stealing, comrade. He may have been given the wire. Or found it.

Investigator   Quite right. Once the crime is proven, we will be obliged to search the scene of the crime in detail – rooting out all unlawful activity –

So. What exactly do the agricultural workers allege?

Vlass (*consulting the charge sheet*)   They saw . . . a number of items disappeared from their stall – knives and so on. This stranger, a tramp, was seen forcing the goods inside his coat. He was followed, he was lost, he was seen again . . .

. . . here, in the market . . .

Investigator   The same man? Just to be clear.

Vlass   A tramp.

(*Again, an idea dawns.*) It could be . . . (another).

Investigator   This man doesn't eat. The rest of us pray for a harvest, even though praying is futile.

Things are not too bad for you market workers, always left-overs coming your way, but for the rest of the people? Thin pickings.

Even so, we are rich beyond belief compared to this man.

Comes to this town, eats little, says nothing.

Look at those arms – like a twist of wire themselves. I've seen more fat on a corpse. Recently.

What work does he do here?

Vlass   Cleans latrines.

Investigator   For how many roubles?

Vlass   I don't *pay* him.

Investigator   Ha – that, comrade, is slavery. Are you telling me this is what the Revolution's come to?

Paulina   He gets food. Good food, I make it myself, with my own hands.

Investigator   Yet he offers no words. No defence, when charged. Guilty, not guilty – all the same to a creature like him. Comes from nowhere, goes nowhere. The man's blood has stopped. It's a miracle his heart beats at all.

If it weren't for the stink because he's here, and the stink in your latrines because he's not there, we wouldn't know he existed . . . But he does exist. I come in the door and wallop, hello, (*sniffing*) something's here. Something that borders on human.

He passes the figure to **Nikita** *through the bars.*

Investigator   Take this back. You at least know what a man looks like.

Or what humans did look like, once.

Let him out.

Vlass   Out, Comrade?!

Investigator   He stinks up my prison cell.

Vlass   Thank you, Comrade Investigator!

Investigator   Let the people decide. A chance to show they give a shit.

As for me, comrade, I have had a very long week. I am going to find a horse, a real horse.

I am going to ride to the other end of town. And then I am going to find a comrade willing, as they say, to offer me a glass of water.

There's a stench in my nose, comrade, like the stench of death. I need to get rid of it – before I forget who *I* am.

He exits. **Vlass** *removes his hat.* **Paulina** *and* **Vlass** *clear stage.* **Nikita** *is left alone. We feel his isolation and exposure.*

Vlass *returns with a mop and bucket, followed by* **Paulina**.

Vlass   Beatings, comrade. Latrine duty, time in chokey – and the company of madmen.

He hands over the mop and bucket. He gives **Nikita** *a friendly slap on the back/shoulder.*

Vlass   Once a soldier, always a soldier, eh.

He exits.

Paulina   Impressive, Croak; all this, and we still don't know who you are.

Must've bin bad, what you left behind.

Nikita *meets her gaze. Lights.*

Eleven

Snow. The sound of sawing. Lights up on the yard. **Dad** *is working with a saw. He is freezing cold. The saw snags on the wood constantly. In a temper, he stops, kicks at the wood. Pauses, begins again.*

Lyuba *enters, wearing her dress and her coat, flapping open.* **Dad** *pauses, looks up, then carries on.*

Lyuba *raises her voice over the noise.*

Lyuba   Father-in-law? I can help. I can saw. Let me saw things.

He stops sawing, looks at her critically.

Dad   A surgeon now, are we?

Lyuba   They sent me home. They say I don't concentrate.

Beat.

Dad   Wash your face. That'd be a start. You're starting to stink, like him.

I'm cutting firewood, that's all.

He starts sawing again. Again she has to speak up.

Lyuba   I can stack wood, I can stitch clothes, I can build bridges, I can plough fields . . . I can fight wars if I have to, I have to do something.

Mikhail!

He stops again. Pause.

Dad   I called by last night. Late on, nine, ten – nothing. That's when it came to me.

Where does a woman in her position go at night? Mmm? You were on the street.

Lyuba   I was looking for Nikita.

Dad   They called it something else in my day.

Lyuba   I'm telling the truth.

Dad   The real Nikita never came back. God knows what it was, the creature you wed. Some ghost or daemon.

He should have stayed on the battlefield, at the front.

Fallen.

Lyuba   You can't say that. Your own son!

Dad   Not natural, the way he was.

My good lads died in the field. I didn't get a body but I got honour. Respect.

Nikit's not the first to kiss the river, someone does it every year. Walk out to the middle, break the ice.

Kiss the river. Always someone takes the easy path.

Lyuba   He wouldn't do that.

He wouldn't do that! How can you . . .

Dad   Your generation don't believe in heaven. Doesn't mean Nikit didn't long for it. Want peace. More than he got with you anyway.

She attempts to grab the saw from him. He pushes her away roughly.

Dad   Stay back, or so help me . . .

Lyuba   Give me work, Mikhail, please, or I will do something terrible.

He saws again, then gives up. He relents, drops the saw, but before leaving checks himself.

Dad   Don't touch the blade. I mean it.

He exits. **Lyuba** *scratches her arm absently, and stares at the saw. She just steps towards it when* **Dad** *returns with a bucket.*

Dad   Here. Straighten them. Ditch the broken ones. Hammer's in the bucket.

Lyuba   Thank you, father-in-law.

Dad *picks up his saw again.*

Lyuba   If he's dead . . .

Dad   He is dead.

Lyuba   Come to the house anytime. If you must. Life goes on.

She turns to exit with the bucket.

Dad   Hey. Where I can watch.

Lyuba   I have to be at home. Grant me that.

Dad   You'd waste your life, Lyuba. That's your generation's talent.

Lyuba   No. Not anymore.

Beat.

Dad *goes back to his sawing.*

Lyuba *pulls a handful of nails from the bucket, lets them drop through her fingers back into the bucket.*

Lyuba   What season is it?

What season . . .

Dad   Spring. Near enough. Thaw's starting.

He takes a drink – or would if the bottle wasn't empty.

I'll be round tonight then.

Lyuba   Fine.

Dad   We'll have a good fire anyway.

Lyuba *exits with the bucket.*

Dad *saws. Lights.*

Twelve

The river. **Lyuba** *steps out onto the ice – putting handfuls of nails from the bucket into her pockets as she goes.*

We hear the sound of creaking ice.

She takes a few finals steps forward, and jumps.

Blackout.

We hear the sound of splintering ice, and a huge splash, **Lyuba***'s gasps – then nothing.*

Thirteen

A block of latrines, all three doors closed. **Nikita** *sweeps his way to the first latrine. He pauses at the door, and knocks.*

Nikita   It's dusk. I lock up the toilets now.

No response. He pushes open the first door – and sweeps. He steps back, and the door of the first cubicle swings closed. He padlocks the door.

He goes to the second door. He pauses at the door, and knocks.

It's dusk. I lock up the toilets now.

A second time, no response. He pushes open the second door – and sweeps. He steps back, and the door of the second cubicle swings closed. He padlocks it.

He steps towards the third cubicle. He knocks . . .

Nikita   It's dusk . . .

Voice (*off*)   Five minutes, comrade.

Nikita *looks along the row, uncertain where the voice came from. He steps forward to the remaining door. He pushes at it, but it is pushed back.*

Voice (*off*)   Jesus Christ, comrade, can a man not take a dump!

Nikita (*very croaky*)   It's dusk. I lock up the toilets now.

Knocks politely.

Voice (*off*)   For God's sake what is it possible to steal in here?

Beat.

Nikita   I lock up the toilets now.

He steps back, waits at a respectable distance. Pause. Silence, as it grows darker. **Dad** *emerges stealthily from the latrine, thinking the attendant has gone. He carries a sack with something in it. With surprise he sees the cleaner, still waiting. He begins to plead.*

Dad   Comrade! I just came for a sack of grain.

I walked twenty versts! Let me get some buckwheat in the morning, then I'll be off. Just a few winks, over here, out of sight. You won't know I'm here. Promise. Out of sight out of mind, eh? For charity's sake. What do you say?

Nikit   It's dusk. I lock up the toilets.

Beat.

Dad *is staring at* **Nikita**.

Dad   Him. You!

Pause.

No no. I should be drinking, I thought . . .

Nikit.

We thought you were . . . he was . . .

We thought you were drowned!

Christ. Peter and Paul, you bastard!

He goes to strike **Nikita**, *but* **Nikita** *is too quick and catches him in a vice-like grip.*

Dad   Oww, oww . . . please!

Nikita *releases him, and stares at his own hand.*

Dad   You're alive!

You're strong!

He begins to laugh/cry with joy.

You'll wear our lives out!

Nikita.

He falls on him, sobbing. **Paulina** *has heard the noise and enters.*

Paulina   Who's that there? Wass going on?

Hey – you alright, Croak?

Dad   I'm his dad!

We thought he was dead!

Paulina   He is pretty much. Now he's alive, you can piss off.

Wake my husband you'll be sorry, I can . . . (tell yer).

Dad   Nikit. Nikit, it's me. Can you hear? It's me, yer dad.

Paulina   Nikit?! I says, 'Is it Nikita?', day one!

Dad   Son!

He embraces **Nikita**. **Nikita** *is at first stiff, then embraces his father.*

Dad   Oh, Nikit. I gave you up!

We searched for hours . . . How did you . . .?

Paulina   Thass enough. Go on now, on yer way . . .

Dad   Lyuba . . . she never gave up. She looked for you all along the river . . .

Paulina   Lyuba? Who's Lyuba?

Dad   She tried to find you, hundred versts, this way, hundred that, find you floating, I don't know. Find you somewhere, surely, a sign, a signal, . . .

Nikita   Lyuba.

Dad   Weighed herself down, through the ice – drowned.

Paulina   Well. She's dead then.

Dad   No – they pulled her out, fishermen from the town.

Nikita   Lyuba.

Dad   Too late, I don't know. A chill, Nikit – she can't shake it. I came to get buckwheat, make some porridge . . .

Nikita   She's alive.

Paulina   What? Everyone's alive now? I can't follow this . . .

Dad   Heal yourself, I says, you're the physician.

Get home, boy.

Paulina   'E bloody well won't get home!

(*Calling.*) Vlass! Vlass! Move yerself!

Dad   You've been here all this while?! Twenty versts away?

Nikita *nods.*

Nikita   I'll go. I'll protect her.

Dad   Go! Find Lyuba.

Paulina   Never mind Lyuba . . .

Dad   I'll come after! Go!

Paulina   You stop there. Croak, don't you dare leave!

He's called Nikita. I can't cope with this no more, I'm losing everything . . .

(*Calling off.*) Vlass, for God's sake!

Bleedin' debt collectin'?!

Nikita *makes to exit.* **Paulina** *steps in.*

Paulina   Oh no.

Dad *puts himself between them.* **Nikita** *exits.*

Dad   Wait, wait. Comrade.

It's alright, comrade. I know I don't look a wealthy man. I know that.

Paulina   Wealthy?

Dad   Look, see? I brought a thing to trade, a clock, a good one, my daughter-in-law's family – no one trusts money now, do they – famine's seen that off.

You fed my son, yes? Cared for him? I'm grateful. Some families, old families, we've still got things from before, things worth something.

Not everything was lost, eh?

No one should be out of pocket for the sake of the Revolution, that's my belief.

Let me pay our debt, mmm?

Take the clock, in exchange, for your trouble, I'll leave it here.

He puts his bag down. At the prospect of money, **Paulina** *is now momentarily undecided – and distracted.*

Dad   There. All yours. Worth a fortune.

Keeps the time n'all. Twice a day.

Fair trade, don't yer say? My lad for a worthless old clock.

Beat. **Dad** *suddenly makes a dash for it, taking the bag with him.*

Paulina   Oy! Oy, come back! Come back!!

Exit **Dad***, pursued by* **Paulina***. Lights.*

Fourteen

Nikita *stumbles home to* **Lyuba***'s house, as it is pieced back together – wardrobe, bed, stove, children's furniture.*

Lights up on **Lyuba** *lying on the bed, wrapped in a blanket, by the stove, which has gone out.*

Noise fades, crossing with dogs barking. Silence.

Nikita *enters upstage. After staring for a while, he calmly takes off his jacket.*

Lyuba*, becoming aware that someone's there, turns her head.*

A long moment.

Lyuba   You.

Pause.

Nikita   Nik / ita

Lyuba   I know.

When did you get . . .

Why are you here?

He steps forward to see her better. She stands.

Lyuba   Don't. Don't speak unless you're staying.

Do you have food, Nikita?

He takes a small loaf from his pocket and puts it in her hands.

They embrace. For a long time they just hold each other.

Eventually she holds him away a little, then she kisses him. He returns the kiss, then oddly it begins to become passionate.

He pulls back, momentarily, ashamed.

Nikita   S-sorry. (*More clearly.*) Sorry.

Lyuba   You want me.

It's alright! I'm your wife, I always wanted you – remember?

Nikita   I kept walking.

Lyuba   I have been so alone, so cold.

He gently pulls her close again, wraps her in the blanket.

Lyuba   Light the stove, make me warm.

Nikita *pulls himself together, goes to light the stove. But there are no sticks/shavings in the bucket. He looks around, spies the little chairs. He takes one.*

Lyuba   No not that . . .

Nikita   There are no children.

He pulls it apart, puts some pieces in the stove, swiftly gets it lit.

Nikita   Paint burns. It'll stink.

Lyuba   It doesn't matter. Come to me.

They wrap themselves together.

I have been so cold.

She coughs.

Nikita   Shhhhh . . .

Lyuba   'Where has he gone?' 'What did I do?'

Nikita   The tramp knew more than I did. I killed him, with a rock.

. . . I cut his head off. It was murder . . .

Lyuba   No no, that was something else.

Nikita   Something else . . .?

Lyuba   Look at me. Look at me!

There is no tramp, Nikit.

Nikita   Yes, a tramp . . .!

Lyuba   Never. Maybe once, but you didn't *do* anything. It was war, Nikit. Something you saw, or . . . It's over now.

You came back too soon, that's all.

Pause.

You'll be alright now, won't you? You won't mind staying with me?

Nikita   I'm used to being happy with you now. I'll stay.

She looks him in the face, strokes it.

Lyuba   Nobody can do anything good on their own.

Nikita   It takes time.

She smiles. And coughs. She loosens the sheet, feverish.

Lyuba   It's hot. I'm too hot.

Nikita   Shhhhh. I know what to do. I'm here.

He pulls the sheet close again, and they remain together, him wrapped around her. They begin to kiss in the glow of the stove.

Dad *enters. He is gasping, winded, but laughing, the clock in the bag still clenched in his hand. He looks off, as if through the window, taking care not to be seen but gesturing crudely to a pursuer, and yelling sotto voce.*

Dad   Yeah, yeah, and fuck you!

Pause for breath. The coast is clear. A beat as he sees the young couple.

Don't mind me.

He laughs as he takes the clock out of the bag, then holds it to his ear.

Peter and Paul . . .! It goes again!

Shit – I forgot the wheat. You don't mind do you?

In the morning I'll go to the river, catch some fish . . . then we'll see what life we have, eh?

Life starts here, comrades, eh?

He sits down on the piano stool, still catching his breath, laughing. Slow fade on **Dad** *and on the couple, as the* **Tramp** *appears, watching the scene, peeling a vegetable with a knife and eating.*

Piano-lesson music drifts in, the (offstage) player, as ever, stumbling to complete the phrase.

Lights.

The End.

Author's note

In 1936 Andrey Platonov started to write a new short story. Called 'The River Potudan', it was set in the aftermath of a brutal civil war that Platonov himself had lived through, more than a decade earlier. Now, seventy years after the author's death, and almost one hundred years since the time in which his story is set, *Bliss* retells that story for the stage.

In the early 1920s, bitter fighting gave way to a famine that affected large swathes of Russia. It was devastating. A seemingly endless scourge destroyed five million people and left many more irreparably scarred. When human flesh is sold openly in street markets, how could it be otherwise?

Where others have written about the power struggles of Russia's leaders at this time, it is the people on the ground, the returning footsoldiers and the remaining civilians scrabbling to survive and to stay human, that Platonov chooses as his focus.

This was Andrey's problem, to be honest. It's the reason that Stalin wrote 'scum' on the back of a magazine bearing one of the few stories Platonov managed to publish in his lifetime. Despite believing passionately in the need for revolution, Platonov couldn't ignore what he saw as the abandonment of the people by those in power. In the 1930s, at a time when Soviet writers were supposed to trumpet socialism's forthcoming and 'inevitable' achievements, Andrey Platonov rubbed his readers' noses in the misery of the-story-so-far – with a bleak and savage humour Samuel Beckett would be proud of.

At the beginning of our play, a young couple think they have survived the war and all it has cost them – and set about making a life together. But they are more damaged than they know. Still, Platonov always believed in the resilience of ordinary people, so by the end of the play – spoiler alert – something has changed in Nikita – and perhaps in Lyuba.

Maybe at last they really have survived; a new beginning becomes possible.

In a similar way, but on a different scale, this production's genesis has been cruelly troubled. When I first read Platonov's story sometime in the noughties, I immediately felt it would make a play for our time. Soldiers returning from war, battling PTSD, trying to put a life together – all this seemed very resonant. No one agreed much. They went on not agreeing for almost a decade. Then Menagerie Theatre in Cambridge presented some scenes in an open workshop as part of their Hotbed Theatre Festival. Finally something began to tick. A year or so later, we premiered the play in Platonov's birthplace of Voronezh, at the annual arts festival held in his name. Personally, I feared we might be drummed out of town for attempting whatever Russians call 'selling coals to Newcastle', but the response was stunning. Our production, we were told, was 'very Russian'. We all, as one, took this as a compliment. A couple of taster dates were played in Cambridge, and a run in London swiftly scheduled for spring 2020.

No doubt you are familiar with what happened next. In the coronavirus pandemic many, many lives have been lost – and are still being lost as I write. The conditions of our lives have altered in weird ways. People – particularly the clinically vulnerable – must wonder if they will ever get the chance to rebuild 'normal' lives. Will the 'before times' ever be recaptured? If they are, what might we discover about the after-effects not only of the virus, but of our trauma? Will we ever feel safe in a crowd again? Will a lover's touch – or a stranger's kiss – ever send the same signal?

Staging the play became impossible during the pandemic. When the lockdown was lifted, the production was rescheduled. Then the context changed a second time, in ways we – in the West at least – had completely failed to imagine.

Putin's unprovoked invasion of Ukraine in February 2022 has brought us daily scenes of the utter inhumanity of war. At the same time, the Ukrainian people show us each day what it means to resist, to remain resilient in the middle of appalling suffering. It is in this capacity for endurance, and the power to overcome, that Platonov always believed.

Like any piece of art, the context changes but the voice remains; our part is to listen, and to live.

FG, May 2022

Acknowledgements

Many thanks to Robert and Elizabeth Chandler and Angela Livingstone, whose translations of Platonov's work (and 'The River Potudan' in particular) have opened up his world to so many, including a monoglot like me. Thanks too to Robbie Aird, Paul Bourne, Ash Day, Lukas Lee, Patrick Morris, Michaela Polakova, Caroline Rippin and Bess Roche – all of whom put so much into bringing this play to life, in what turned out to be a much-longer-than-anticipated R&D phase.

www.ingramcontent.com/pod-product-compliance
Ingram Content Group UK Ltd.
Pitfield, Milton Keynes, MK11 3LW, UK
UKHW020709280225
455688UK00012B/328

9 781350 346239